D1404535

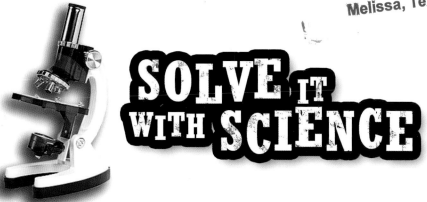

SOLVE IT WITH SCIENCE

VIOLENT CRIMES

JON SUTHERLAND
AND
DIANE CANWELL

A⁺
Smart Apple Media

This book has been published in cooperation with Arcturus Publishing Limited.

The right of Jon Sutherland and Diane Canwell to be identified as the authors of this work has been asserted by them in accordance with the Copyright, Designs and Patents Act 1988.

Series concept: Alex Woolf
Editor and picture researcher: Alex Woolf
Designer: Tall Tree

The illustrations on pages 32, 34 and 38 are by Jason Line.

Copyright © 2009 Arcturus Publishing Limited

Published in the United States by Smart Apple Media
P.O. Box 3263, Mankato, Minnesota 56002

Printed in China

Library of Congress Cataloging-in-Publication Data

Sutherland, Jonathan.
  Violent crimes / Jon Sutherland and Diane Canwell.
    p. cm. – (Solve it with science)
  Includes index.
  ISBN 978-1-59920-334-8 (hardcover)
  1. Violent crimes–United States–Juvenile literature. I. Canwell, Diane. II. Title.
  HV6789.S953 2010
  364.152'3092273–dc22
                                        2009002018

9 8 7 6 5 4 3 2 1

All words in **bold** may be found in the glossary on pages 46–47.

CONTENTS

INTRODUCTION 4

THE JIGSAW MURDERS 8

THE ACID BATH MURDERS 12

BORN TO RAISE HELL 16

TED BUNDY 20

THE WOOD CHIPPER 24

THE NIGHT STALKER 28

HOLLYWOOD MURDER MYSTERY 32

BUG EVIDENCE 36

MURDER AT THE PIG FARM 40

TIME LINE 44

GLOSSARY 46

FURTHER INFORMATION 47

INDEX 48

INTRODUCTION

When someone uses force on a victim, this is a violent crime. Murder, robbery, assault, and kidnapping are all violent crimes. Such crimes often involve the use of a gun or a knife. The most serious type of violent crime is murder—the killing of another human being.

FAMOUS VIOLENT CRIMES

History is littered with violent crimes. In nineteenth-century Scotland, William Burke and William Hare murdered people to sell the bodies to doctors for medical experiments.

In the United States in the 1920s, gangsters were involved in many violent crimes. One of the most famous, and violent, gangsters was Al Capone.

Murderers often make great efforts to remove the evidence of their crimes.

There were violent gangsters in London, too. In the 1960s, the Kray twins and the Richardson family were involved in hijacks, armed robbery, and gang killings.

Not all violent crimes are carried out for money. Beverley Allitt, a nurse in England, became known as the Angel of Death. She killed four small children in the 1990s. Her motives for doing so have never fully been understood.

Some commit violent crimes for love. Ruth Ellis shot and killed her boyfriend after an argument. Hanged in 1955, she was the last woman in England to face the death penalty.

FORENSICS AND VIOLENT CRIME
Many different **forensic** techniques are used to help solve violent crimes. Forensic scientists may be able to find evidence at the crime scene. They are specially trained to look for things that other people may not even notice.

SERIAL KILLERS

Among the most notorious violent crimes are those carried out by **serial killers**. Dennis Nilson, for example, killed 15 people in five years. Peter Sutcliffe, who murdered 13 women over six years, became known as the Yorkshire Ripper.

Peter Sutcliffe killed 13 women and attacked several others in West Yorkshire, UK, between 1975 and 1981.

At crime scenes, there may be fingerprints, footprints, tire tracks, chips of paint, soil, and fibers. There may be biological evidence such as blood, hair, or fingernails. Forensic scientists may find evidence of the weapon that was used—bullets or knife marks. All of these clues are known as **trace evidence** and are very important in solving violent crimes.

Samples of trace evidence are collected by brushing, vacuuming, or swabbing the crime scene. Samples are collected in bags, carefully labeled, and then taken to the laboratory. Forensic scientists then analyze the samples to help them understand what happened and who may have committed the crime.

IDENTIFYING VICTIMS AND SUSPECTS

If the crime scene is old, then other forensic techniques can be used. **Forensic anthropology** involves the study of skeletons and other human remains to discover the identity of a victim.

Sometimes, forensic dentistry is used to identify victims. A victim's teeth can be compared with the dental records of missing people to try to find a match. **Forensic odontologists** can also help to

Forensic scientists search for evidence at a crime scene. They wear protective clothing, gloves, and masks to ensure they don't contaminate the evidence.

A forensic entomologist uses a microscope to analyze a fly found on the body of a murder victim.

identify a suspect from teeth marks that have been left on a victim or in discarded food found at the crime scene.

TIME, PLACE, AND CAUSE OF DEATH

Forensic entomology is the study of insects found in or around a body to establish the time or place of death. **Pathologists** try to discover the cause of death by examining the bodies of victims.

DNA PROFILING

DNA is the chemical material that holds the code for every cell in a person's body. DNA is like a fingerprint—everyone's DNA is slightly different. Every cell in your body, including blood, saliva, skin, and hair, contains DNA. It can be gathered from eating utensils, clothing, and other items found at crime scenes. DNA profiling was developed in the 1980s. Since then, it has provided vital evidence in many cases by linking suspects to crime scenes.

THE JIGSAW MURDERS

Buck Ruxton was born in Bombay, India, in 1899. In 1930, he moved to Lancaster in the UK and set himself up as a doctor. He married a woman named Isabella who was a sociable and popular lady in the community.

Dr. Buck Ruxton was a respected doctor and well liked by his patients.

THE JEALOUS DOCTOR

Ruxton was jealous of his wife's popularity and came to believe she was having an affair. On September 15, 1935, he strangled Isabella. Because her maid Mary Rogerson had witnessed his crime, he killed her too. He cut the bodies up, put them in his car, then drove through the night to Scotland, about 100 miles (160 km) to the north. He dumped the body parts in a stream.

THE OBSERVANT CYCLIST

On his return journey from Scotland, Ruxton knocked over a cyclist named Bernard Beattie. Ruxton did not stop, but the cyclist wrote down the car's license plate. The registration matched Ruxton's. The doctor later denied he had driven to Scotland that night, but Beattie's statement provided strong evidence to the contrary.

Mary Rogerson's mother reported her missing to the police. They visited Ruxton to ask about her, but he said she had not been to work for two days. A few days later, the police returned to Ruxton because Isabella's friends had reported her missing. He told the police that Isabella had gone away with her lover.

SURPRISE PACKAGE

Not long afterward, body remains were found in a ravine in Moffat, Scotland. The body parts were wrapped in a copy of a newspaper that was only sold in Lancashire—a

vital clue that the police were quick to follow up on. The body parts were sent to the University of Edinburgh for an **autopsy** examination. It was established that the bodies belonged to two women, one a young lady and the other in her forties.

Police search for evidence at the ravine in Moffat, Scotland, where the two bodies were discovered.

The tips of the women's fingers had been removed to prevent fingerprint identification. However, police suspected that the dead bodies belonged to the missing women, Isabella Ruxton and Mary Rogerson. It was now up to forensic scientists to prove it.

NEW TECHNIQUES

A team of forensic scientists was assembled, led by pathologist John Glaister and **anatomist** James Couper Brash. They used several new techniques to match the remains to the two women.

The scientists decided to reconstruct the bodies. They did this by matching each body part to any known distinguishing features of the women. They **x-rayed** the skulls and then **superimposed** tracings from photographs of each woman on the x-rays. Eventually, they managed to reconstruct two skeletons from the various body parts. Because the jumbled body parts had to be reassembled like a jigsaw puzzle, the case became known as the "jigsaw murders."

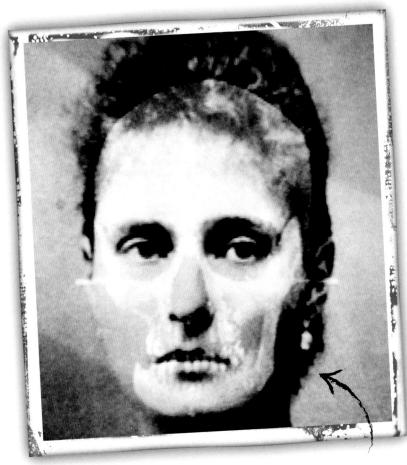

Forensic scientists used techniques similar to those employed in the Buck Ruxton case to match skull fragments to Tsarina Alexandra of Russia (1872–1918). A photo of the tsarina was superimposed on an x-ray of the skull fragments.

PHOTOGRAPHING THE SKULLS

Professor Brash came up with the idea of x-raying the skulls. He had photographs of Isabella and Mary enlarged to life size. This allowed him to trace the facial characteristics of each of the women onto transparent paper. By placing the transparent paper over the x-rays, he could match the facial characteristics of the two women to the x-rays of the skulls.

The scientists also used forensic entomology—the study of insects in criminal investigations—a science in its infancy in 1935. Insect larvae found in the body parts were taken to the laboratory and the larvae's age was established. The age fit perfectly with the date that the bodies had been dumped.

A blowfly larva feeds on liver tissue.
The length of the blowfly's life cycle from egg to fly varies according to temperature, so the size of the larva and temperature can be used to calculate time of death.

TRIAL

Ruxton was arrested on October 13. During the trial, Glaister and Brash gave their evidence. It was the first time their pioneering forensic techniques had been used as evidence in a court of law. The forensic evidence proved to be crucial. Buck Ruxton was found guilty of murdering the two women. He was hanged in Manchester on May 12, 1936.

THE ACID BATH MURDERS

John George Haigh was born in Yorkshire, UK, in 1909. During his 20s and early 30s, he went to prison several times for fraud and theft. After his 1944 release from prison, he started to commit murders.

John George Haigh, the Acid Bath Murderer

DISPOSING OF THE BODIES

On September 9, 1944, Haigh hit his employer and friend William McSwan over the head and slit his throat. Haigh put the body in a large metal drum and filled it with concentrated **sulfuric acid**. He wore a gas mask and rubber clothes to protect himself from the acid. By the following day, the body had turned to sludge, which Haigh poured down a drain.

Haigh told McSwan's parents that their son had gone to Scotland. When the parents became suspicious, he killed them, on July 2, 1945, and dissolved their bodies in acid. He forged William McSwan's signature on legal documents so he could sell the McSwan family possessions and receive their pensions. Haigh moved into an expensive hotel, the Onslow Court, in Kensington, London.

THE EFFECTS OF ACID

Haigh believed that dissolving his victims in acid would destroy any evidence of the bodies. But he was wrong. Certain parts of the human body, such as bone and fat, do not dissolve so quickly or easily. Also, artificial items belonging to his victims, such as false teeth, were discovered and used as evidence by forensic scientists.

MORE VICTIMS

An addicted gambler, Haigh soon began to run out of money. He looked for someone else to kill and steal from. In 1947, he befriended Dr. Archibald Henderson and his wife Rose. In February 1948, he shot them both. Again, he dissolved both bodies in acid. Haigh forged documents to get the couple's money. Then, at Onslow Court, he met a wealthy elderly woman, Mrs. Olive Durand-Deacon. Very soon she was also dead.

Dr. Archibald and Rose Henderson were victims of Haigh.

13

ARRESTED

Haigh sold Durand-Deacon's jewelry and fur coat. Constance Lane, a friend of Durand-Deacon, reported her disappearance to the police. The police interviewed people at the hotel. They soon discovered Haigh's criminal record and became suspicious. The police searched Haigh's storehouse in Crawley. They found a revolver and eight bullets. On March 2, 1949, Haigh was arrested.

Dr. Keith Simpson, a government pathologist, searched for evidence in a pile of burned garbage at Haigh's Crawley storehouse.

Haigh confessed to the killings. He told the police he had dissolved the bodies in acid after drinking their blood. Several doctors and psychologists had interviewed him about his claims of needing to drink blood. They decided he had committed the murders for his own gains and had pretended to be insane when he was caught.

REMAINS DISCOVERED

Despite Haigh's efforts to dissolve the bodies, traces of human remains were found by forensic scientists. These included body fat and fragments of bone. Part of Durand-Deacon's left foot was discovered and a cast was made

HOSPITAL VISIT

Two days after the murders, Speck was admitted to Cook County Hospital. He had attempted suicide with an overdose of drugs. He was treated by Dr. LeRoy Smith, who recognized Speck from the drawing the police had circulated. He also recognized the tattoo on Speck's arm. Dr. Smith contacted the police.

Speck was arrested and charged with eight counts of murder. He remained in the hospital under police guard. The police arranged for Corazon Amurao to dress as a nurse and go into Speck's room. She identified Speck as the intruder and murderer.

TRIAL AND SENTENCE

Before Speck's trial could begin, he was examined by eight independent psychiatrists. The psychiatrists reported that Speck was fit to stand trial. Speck's trial began on February 20, 1967. He was found guilty and sentenced to death. In 1972, his sentence was changed to life imprisonment. Speck died in prison in December 1991.

Corazon Amurao (left), *the sole survivor of Speck's attack, was reunited with her family.*

TED BUNDY

In 1946, Theodore "Ted" Bundy was born near Philadelphia, Pennsylvania. He may be America's most infamous serial killer. Bundy embarked on his killing spree in 1974 while studying law at the University of Washington in Seattle. Between January and July 1974, nine young girls—most of them students—disappeared in Seattle.

Mass murderer Ted Bundy

MAN WITH A SLING

In July, witnesses gave police a description of a man with a sling who had approached a young girl in a park. A forensic artist drew an impression of the man from these descriptions. It was published in Seattle newspapers. Several people who knew Ted Bundy reported him as a possible suspect. However, these were just a few out of thousands of responses, and the police did not follow up on the lead.

On September 6, 1974, some human remains were discovered near Seattle. Dental records helped to identify the remains as belonging to Janice Ott and Denise Laslund, two of the missing girls.

UTAH AND COLORADO

By this time, Bundy had moved to Salt Lake City, Utah, where he attended the University of Utah law school. The disappearances soon began again. Four girls were reported missing between October and December 1974.

In 1975, Bundy shifted his murderous activities to Colorado. Between January and July, nine girls, between ages 13 and 24, disappeared. Some of the girls vanished without a trace. The bodies of the others were discovered. They showed signs of having been severely beaten and strangled.

In Colorado, Bundy was arrested and convicted of kidnapping and assaulting Carol DaRonch. She was one of the few to survive an encounter with Bundy and was able to identify him. The police also hoped to charge him with the murder of another girl, Caryn Campbell, whose hair was found to be very similar to a hair found in Bundy's car.

These are highly magnified shafts of human hair. Hair experts are skilled at recognizing the individual characteristics of different people's hair.

HAIR IDENTIFICATION

Human hair has a number of distinctive features, including length, color, thickness, and root appearance. Forensic scientists use a **comparison microscope** to try to match hair from a crime scene with hair from a suspect or victim. Although human hair shares many of the same qualities, a skilled hair examiner can see microscopic differences between hairs belonging to different people.

21

TO FLORIDA

While Bundy was awaiting trial for murder, he managed to escape from prison and fled to Florida. He soon continued his killing spree by murdering three more girls and maiming three others.

A woman named Nita Neary witnessed a man leaving the homes of Lisa Levy and Martha Bowman, two of Bundy's victims, on January 15, 1978. Neary called the police, who found the bodies of the two girls in their beds. The police could find no fingerprints in the room. But they did find a bite mark on Lisa Levy. This proved to be a crucial piece of evidence.

ARREST AND TRIAL

Ted Bundy was arrested on February 15, 1978. He went on trial in June 1979. Nita Neary's positive identification of Bundy and the bite mark on Lisa Levy helped to establish his guilt.

Dr. Richard Souviron, a forensic odontologist, gave evidence in court. He showed the jury an enlarged photo of the bite mark. He laid over it a transparent sheet with an enlarged photo of Bundy's teeth. Some of his teeth were chipped or unevenly aligned. It was obvious to the jury that Bundy's distinctive teeth matched the bite mark.

Carol DaRonch, who survived an attack by Bundy, gives evidence at his trial.

Ted Bundy was found guilty and sentenced to death. Bundy was executed in Florida in January 1989. Before he died, he confessed to 30 murders.

FORENSIC DENTISTRY

The Ted Bundy case was the first time that evidence obtained through forensic dentistry had been used in a Florida court. Forensic odontologists compare the dental impressions taken from someone's mouth with bite mark impressions on the skin. They look for similar indents, pits, and cuts. Often, this is done through computer-enhanced photography. They can also analyze bite marks on food in cases where a burglar has taken a bite out of food in a victim's house.

Bundy claimed that he chipped his tooth in March 1978, after killing Lisa Levy, so the odontologist's evidence was wrong. But this photo, taken in August 1977, clearly shows Bundy with a chipped tooth.

THE WOOD CHIPPER

Richard Crafts was born in New York City, in 1937. He grew up to become an airline pilot. In 1975, he married a Danish-born stewardess named Helle. They bought a house in Newtown, Connecticut, and had three children. But things were not good. Richard was having affairs with other women. In 1986, Helle decided she wanted a divorce and employed Keith Mayo, a private detective, to find evidence that Richard was having an affair.

Richard Crafts

VANISHED

On November 20, 1986, Helle went missing. However, Crafts did not report her disappearance to the police. Keith Mayo was convinced that Helle would not just disappear. He contacted the local police.

When questioned by the police, Crafts claimed that he and Helle had argued, and she had walked out. However, Crafts told different things to different people. He told the au pair, Dawn Thomas, that Helle had gone to Denmark to be with her sick mother.

SEARCHING THE HOUSE

Their suspicions aroused, the police obtained a warrant to search the couple's home. They were astounded by what they found. Crafts possessed a large number of pistols, handguns, hand grenades, and ammunition. The police took away the weapons, as well as towels, samples of fibers, and a mattress for closer examination. Forensic scientist Dr. Henry Lee carried out a **luminal test** in various parts of the house. It tested positive for the presence of blood.

Back at his laboratory, Dr. Lee tested the towels and bedding. He found samples of type O-positive blood—the same **blood type** as Helle. But the police could do nothing without Helle's body.

LUMINAL TEST

To carry out a luminal test, a **serologist** (blood specialist) sprays an area with special chemicals. In the dark, the sprayed area turns bright blue if blood is present. The luminal test is highly sensitive and can even detect blood that has been diluted in water.

Private investigator Keith Mayo was the first to raise the alarm about the disappearance of Helle Crafts.

A WITNESS

A breakthrough occurred on December 30. A snowplow driver, Joseph Hine, told police he had seen someone using a wood chipper near the river close to Crafts's house on the night of November 20. Detectives had already learned from Crafts's credit card statements that he had rented a wood chipper in a nearby town on November 19.

GRUESOME FINDS

The police thoroughly searched the area where the wood chipper had been seen. They found 56 tiny fragments of bone, cloth, hair, a piece of a toe, a fragment of fingernail, and a letter. In the river, they found strands of blonde hair and a chainsaw.

The police arrested Crafts in January 1987. The forensic team's research indicated that Crafts had killed his wife in the bedroom and then froze her body in the basement freezer. After cutting her body up with the chainsaw, he had taken the pieces to the wood chipper and shredded her. Because the wood chipper was close to the river, the bulk of her remains had blown into the water.

FORENSIC EVIDENCE

Dr. Lee testified at Crafts's trial. Forensic tests proved that the pieces of bone, hair, tissue, and nail had been shredded using the same wood chipper.

In the teeth of the chainsaw, scientists found strands of Helle's hair and fibers that matched a rug from their home. The chainsaw's serial number matched the one that Richard Crafts had bought in 1981.

Crafts rented a wood chipper similar to this one.

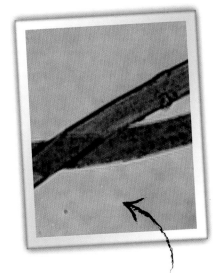

FIBER ANALYSIS

Forensic scientists use various tests to try to match fibers. First, color and physical appearance are compared using a comparison microscope. The test is then repeated under different kinds of light. Sometimes colors can appear the same in ordinary light, but differences show up under **infrared** and **ultraviolet** light. **Infrared spectrometry** is the most precise test. It measures the amount of infrared light that is absorbed when it passes through a fiber. If the results are the same for two fibers, scientists have found a definite match.

Magnified photos of clothing fibers found at a crime scene. The fibers can be compared to fiber samples taken from the suspect.

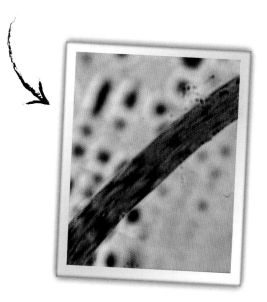

TRIAL AND SENTENCE

In 1990, Richard Crafts was found guilty of murder and sentenced to 99 years imprisonment.

THE NIGHT STALKER

Richard Ramirez was born in El Paso, Texas, in 1960. In his teens, he became a heavy drug user and petty thief. In 1978, he moved to California. Six years later, Ramirez began to kill people.

Richard Ramirez, known as the Night Stalker

FIRST VICTIM

His first murder occured on June 28, 1984. The victim was Jennie Vincow, aged 79. Ramirez stabbed her to death in her apartment in Los Angeles, California. Police found fingerprints on the windowsill, but no other leads.

ON THE RAMPAGE

On March 17, 1985, Ramirez struck again. He accosted Angela Barrios in the garage of her apartment building in Los Angeles. Angela was lucky to survive.

Ramirez shot at her, but the keys she was holding deflected the bullet. Her roommate, Dayle Okazaki, was not so fortunate. Ramirez shot her in the head. The police found Ramirez's baseball cap in their garage.

That same night, Ramirez killed Tsia-Lian Yu. He pulled her out of her car in Monterey Park, California, and shot her. The police retrieved a metal

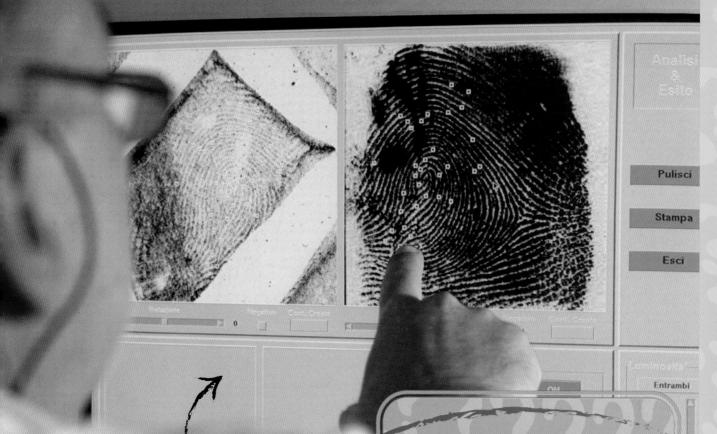

Pulisci

Stampa

Esci

A forensic scientist uses a computer to analyze the features of a fingerprint—indicated by the yellow spots.

medallion and a torn section of a $20 bill from the crime scene. Three days later, Ramirez murdered an eight-year-old girl in Eagle Rock, California.

A week later, Ramirez killed Peter and Maxine Zazzara in their home in Whittier, California. The police found footprints of a tennis shoe in the gardens outside their home.

FINGERPRINT EVIDENCE

Sweat, body oils, and dirt mix to leave latent fingerprints on smooth surfaces. Fingerprint identification and matching has been greatly helped by computers. Fingerprints can be analyzed and compared with millions of other fingerprints in a computer database in a matter of minutes. Computers can also be programmed to draw a complete fingerprint from fragments.

In May, Ramirez attacked Harold and Jean Wu. Harold died in the hospital from a gunshot wound, but Jean survived and gave the police a physical description of Ramirez.

THE KILLINGS CONTINUE

Ramirez continued attacking and killing throughout the summer. He became known in Los Angeles as the Night Stalker.

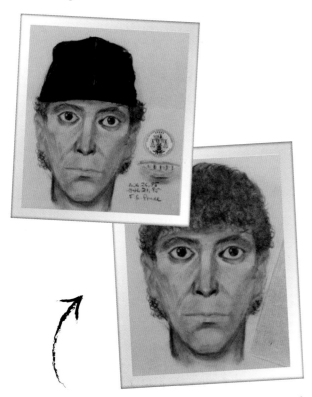

The Los Angeles police released a composite drawing of Ramirez based on Jean Wu's description.

Ramirez moved to San Francisco, California. On August 18, he shot Peter and Barbara Pan in the head and wrote "Jack the Knife" on their wall in lipstick. The forensic team removed a bullet from Peter's head and sent it to the forensic team in Los Angeles. The bullet matched those they had removed from Ramirez's Los Angeles victims.

One of his victims survived the attack and saw Ramirez leaving the crime scene in an orange Toyota car. She noted the license plate number and reported it to the police. When the police found the car, a forensic team searched it for evidence and found a fingerprint. It matched the fingerprint records of Ramirez. The print also matched the one on Jennie Vincow's windowsill from 1984.

CAPTURED

Finally, on August 31, 1985, the police tracked Ramirez down in Los Angeles. They had been alerted by residents who recognized his face from a photo published in the newspapers.

RESTRICTION FRAGMENT LENGTH POLYMORPHISM

Restriction fragment length polymorphism (RFLP) is a technique used to analyze a DNA sample. Special proteins called restriction enzymes break up the sample into fragments. Each fragment is a DNA sequence, a particular ordering of the chemicals within DNA. Analyzing these sequences helps to identify a DNA sample or match it to another one.

TRIAL AND SENTENCE

At his trial, the **prosecution** described the most likely scenario. David Minor had broken into Roland Kuster's house intending to steal something. But Kuster had disturbed him and a fight had broken out. Minor had killed Kuster and fled the scene, but he forgot to take his backpack. This, and Minor's blood found at the scene, was enough to convict him. He was found guilty and sentenced to life imprisonment.

This DNA sequence has been produced using RFLP.

BUG EVIDENCE

On July 9, 1997, Kevin Neal reported to the police that his two children were missing. He told them that India (11) and Cody (4) had been playing in the yard of his house in Champaign County, Ohio.

GROWING SUSPICIONS

The police began searching the area but could find no sign of the children. There had been family problems, and the police were suspicious that Kevin Neal or his wife were responsible for the children's disappearance. The police interviewed the neighbors. They had not heard the children playing outside that day.

Neal told the police that his car did not work. He said he had not driven it for more than a month. But neighbors confirmed that it had not been in the driveway on the day the children disappeared.

Another reason to suspect Neal was his criminal past. He had twice been convicted of assaults on women.

A GRISLY DISCOVERY

On September 6, Andrew Stickley was working on his farm in Nettle Creek, Ohio. As his tractor passed near a cemetery bordering the farm, Stickley detected the smell of decay. He went into the cemetery to investigate and discovered the bodies of two children. Stickley called the police. The bodies were soon identified as those of India and Cody.

The seeds found on Neal's jeans came from Kentucky bluegrass, which grew at the Nettle Creek cemetery, but not at Neal's residence.

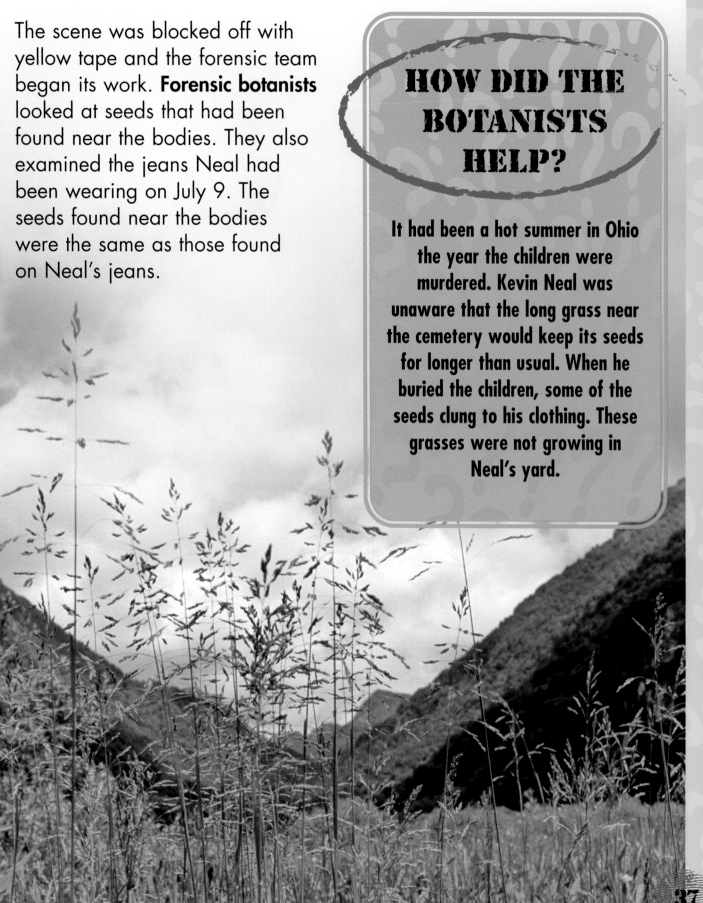

The scene was blocked off with yellow tape and the forensic team began its work. **Forensic botanists** looked at seeds that had been found near the bodies. They also examined the jeans Neal had been wearing on July 9. The seeds found near the bodies were the same as those found on Neal's jeans.

HOW DID THE BOTANISTS HELP?

It had been a hot summer in Ohio the year the children were murdered. Kevin Neal was unaware that the long grass near the cemetery would keep its seeds for longer than usual. When he buried the children, some of the seeds clung to his clothing. These grasses were not growing in Neal's yard.

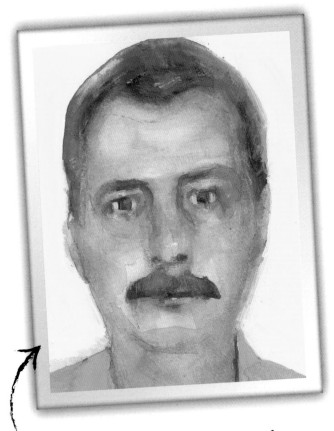

Kevin Neal was a suspect from the start of the investigation.

STUDYING THE INSECTS

Forensic entomologists analyzed the insects found inside and around the bodies. By measuring the stages these insects had reached in their life cycles, the entomologists could calculate how long they had been living on the bodies and establish the approximate time of death.

Establishing the time of death was critical in this case. If the children had died after the end of July,

Neal could not have been the killer, as he would have been in prison. Three weeks after the children disappeared, Neal had been sent to prison for assaulting a woman.

The police warned the media that the forensic analysis could take months. But they were not in any hurry because Kevin Neal, their chief suspect, was behind bars. The case finally went to trial in May 2000.

TIME OF DEATH

Forensic entomologist Dr. Neal Haskell gave evidence at the trial. He was one of the first people to apply entomology to criminal investigations. Haskell explained to the jury how the life cycle of a fly can help to establish the time of death. Based on his analysis of the insects at the crime scene, he said that the children had died between July 9–14, 1997.

SENTENCE

The jury found Neal guilty of murder. He was sentenced to life imprisonment.

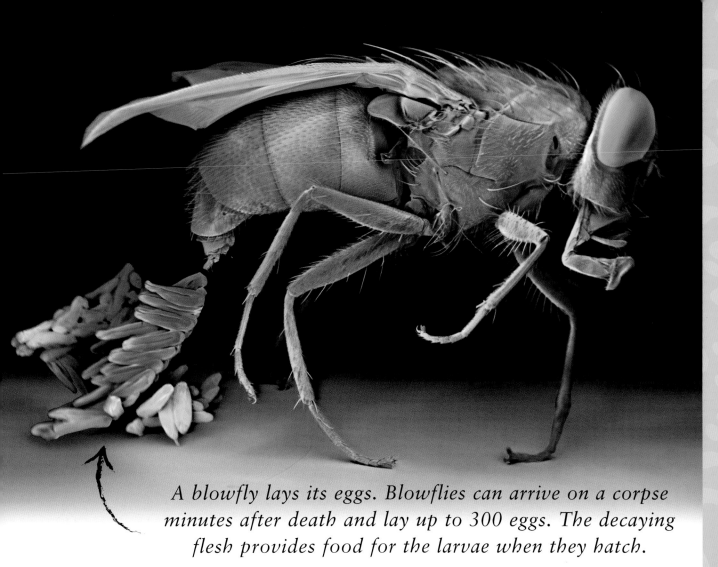

A blowfly lays its eggs. Blowflies can arrive on a corpse minutes after death and lay up to 300 eggs. The decaying flesh provides food for the larvae when they hatch.

WHAT IS FORENSIC ENTOMOLOGY?

Forensic entomologists use their knowledge of insects' life cycles and behavior to establish time of death. Certain insects, such as blowflies, cheese skippers, and screwworms, are attracted to decomposing bodies. Each type of insect prefers bodies at different stages of decomposition. The speed of their life cycles varies according to the average external temperature. The forensic entomologist takes all of these factors into account when calculating time of death.

MURDER AT THE PIG FARM

During the 1980s and 1990s, many women were reported missing in British Columbia, Canada. Approximately 60 women vanished between 1983 and 2001. In 1998, the Vancouver Police Department set up a special team to investigate the disappearances.

One member of the team, Inspector Kim Rossmo, used a **geographic profiling** technique to map the disappearances of the women and search for any patterns. In 1999, Rossmo reported an unusually high concentration of disappearances in downtown Eastside. This suggested that a serial killer might be at work.

THE PIG FARMER

One of several police suspects was Robert Pickton, who owned

Robert Pickton, a local pig farmer, held wild parties in a converted building at his farm to which a number of the missing women had been invited.

a pig farm in Port Coquitlam, British Columbia. Pickton had been charged with the attempted murder of a woman in 1997.

On February 5, 2002, the local police decided to search Pickton's farm after witnesses reported that he kept illegal firearms there.

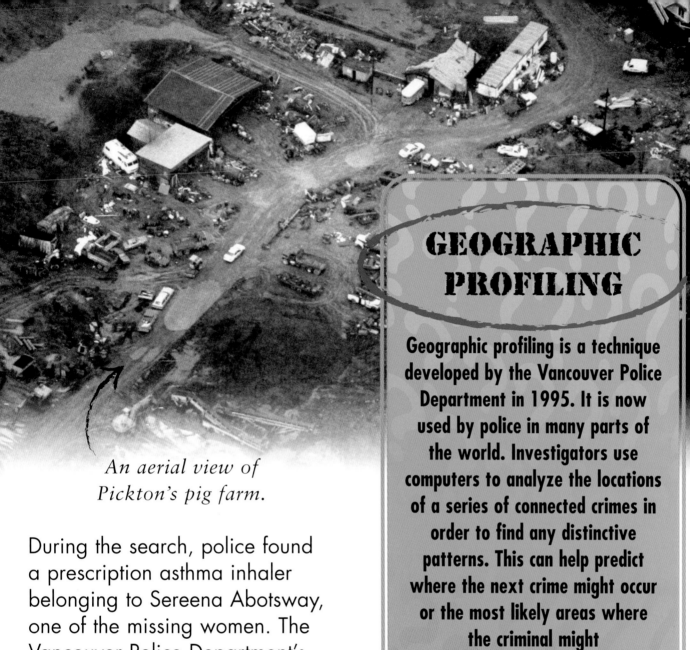

An aerial view of Pickton's pig farm.

During the search, police found a prescription asthma inhaler belonging to Sereena Abotsway, one of the missing women. The Vancouver Police Department's team was contacted. Robert Pickton was arrested and charged with murder.

GEOGRAPHIC PROFILING

Geographic profiling is a technique developed by the Vancouver Police Department in 1995. It is now used by police in many parts of the world. Investigators use computers to analyze the locations of a series of connected crimes in order to find any distinctive patterns. This can help predict where the next crime might occur or the most likely areas where the criminal might be found.

THE FORENSIC TEAM MOVES IN

The forensic team began the task of searching Pickton's 14 acre (5.7 ha) farm for evidence. Very soon, they began to unearth human remains. As these were identified as the missing women, Pickton was charged with more and more murders. By October 2002, he had been accused of 15 murders.

41

Excavations continued until October 2004. Investigators found thousands of pieces of evidence at the farm. Other forensic experts focused on reconstructing the crime scene by looking at how the bones were scattered around the farm.

THE TRIAL BEGINS

By the time Pickton's trial began in January 2006, he had been charged with 27 murders. However, the judge reduced the number of charges to 6. He decided that trying all 27 would be unfair on the jury as it could take up to two years.

The prosecution alleged that Pickton took the women to his home in Port Coquitlam, murdered them, butchered their remains, and then disposed of them. The jury was presented with a great deal of forensic evidence. Human bones, blood, teeth, and hair had been found on the pig farm. Forensic anthropologists were able to match the DNA found in these samples to the DNA of many of the missing women.

INSECT EVIDENCE

A forensic entomologist, Dr. Gail Anderson, also gave evidence. By analyzing the insects found in the remains of two of the women, she was able to show that they had been left out in the open for several weeks or months before being placed in the freezer where they were found. Insects had entered the remains before they were put into the freezer. The type of insect and their stage of development helped scientists date the deaths.

In their search for evidence, investigators used conveyor belts to sift through large quantities of earth at Pickton's farm.

TEETH AND DNA

Some of the murder victims on Pickton's farm were identified by their teeth. Teeth are a good source of DNA. The enamel protects the inside of the tooth. When the inside is mixed with liquid nitrogen, it can be crushed to produce a fine powder. This powder can then be tested for DNA.

SENTENCE

In December 2007, Pickton's trial ended. The jury found Pickton guilty and the judge sentenced him to life imprisonment with no chance of parole for 25 years.

A scientist removes tissue from a tooth in order to extract a sample of the DNA.

43

TIME LINE

1835   Henry Goddard of Britain's Scotland Yard is the first to prove a bullet was fired from a particular gun.

1884   The first use of forensic evidence occurs in a violent crimes case. John Toms shot a man with a pistol. The wound in the victim's head contained newspaper. This newspaper was matched to some found in Toms's pockets.

1889   French professor Alexandre Lacassagne links a bullet from a murder scene with a revolver by counting the number of grooves in the revolver's barrel and matching this to marks on the bullet.

1891   Austrian Hans Gross suggests that traces of hair, dust, footprints, and fibers can help track down a criminal.

1892   Sir Francis Galton publishes *Finger Prints*, which describes different patterns of fingerprints and shows that no two people have the same fingerprints.

1892   Fingerprint evidence is used in a trial in Argentina to convict a woman of murdering her children.

1897   Edward Richard Henry solves a murder in India by proving that a bloody thumbprint belongs to the murderer.

1901   German scientist Paul Uhlenhuth discovers a means of distinguishing human blood from animal blood.

1901   Karl Landsteiner of Austria discovers the different blood types.

1904   In the first case solved by trace evidence, German scientist Georg Popp proves that Karl Laubach committed murder based on the evidence of a handkerchief left at the scene.

1910 Edmond Locard sets up the first police crime laboratory in France.

1910 Rosella Rousseau is convicted of murdering Germaine Bichon because of hair found at the crime scene. Victor Balthazard, the French medical examiner, proves that the hair Bichon was clutching came from Rousseau's head.

1913 Victor Balthazard makes advances in bullet identification. He is the first to use enlarged photographs to identify bullets.

1915 Italian Leone Lattes finds a way of testing the blood type of dried blood.

1936 On the basis of hair and fiber evidence, John Fiorenza is found guilty of murdering New York writer Nancy Evans Titterton.

1977 The world's first computerized fingerprint database is established in the United States.

1983–4 DNA testing is developed in the United States and Britain.

1987 Colin Pitchfork of Britain, who murdered two girls, is the first criminal to be convicted through DNA evidence.

1990s The National Integrated Ballistic Identification Network (NIBIN), a national database for identifying bullets and guns, is developed in the United States.

1991 Canada develops the first Integrated Ballistics Imaging System (IBIS). It compares the different marks on bullets and shells.

1998 American scientists create the Combined DNA Index System. This allows crime laboratories across the United States to compare DNA samples with a national database.

GLOSSARY

anatomist
An expert in the physical structure of the human body.

autopsy
An examination of a dead body in order to establish cause and circumstances of death.

ballistics
The study of firearms and ammunition.

blood type
Any of several groups into which human blood is divided based on inherited properties.

comparison microscope
A microscope that shows two things at the same time so that they can be compared.

composite drawing
A drawing made up of several elements.

DNA
A chemical molecule that carries genetic information; everyone's DNA is slightly different, and it can be used to identify a particular individual.

forensics
The scientific analysis of physical evidence.

forensic anthropology
The application of the study of the human skeleton to criminal investigations. Forensic anthropologists help to identify human remains by using their expertise to establish things such as sex, age, and health.

forensic artists
Artists who use their skills to help in a criminal investigation. They can produce composite drawings from witness descriptions, age progressions from photos, and facial reconstructions from skeletal remains.

forensic botanists
Scientists who apply the study of plant life to criminal investigations. Forensic botanists examine leaves, seeds, and pollen found at crime scenes to determine time frames and whether a body has been moved between different locations. They can also match plant fragments to those found on a suspect.

forensic entomology
The application of the study of insect life to criminal investigations. Forensic entomologists examine insects found in and around dead bodies in order to establish time and place of death.

forensic odontologist
Forensic odontologists, or dentists, can help to identify human remains by matching teeth to existing dental records. They are also able to match bite marks, for example, in food discarded at a crime scene, to the teeth of suspects.

gallstone
A small hard mass that forms inside the gallbladder, often as a result of infection. The gallbladder is a small muscular sac that forms part of the human digestive system.

geographic profiling
A technique that uses computers to map locations of similar crimes in order to figure out where the criminal is located or might strike next.

infrared
Radiation (energy waves) with wavelengths longer than visible light but shorter than radio waves.

infrared spectrometry
A method used to measure how much infrared light is absorbed when passing through a transparent substance. This measurement is known as a signature and can be compared to the signatures of other known substances to identify the unknown substance.

luminal test
A test used to detect the presence of blood on a piece of material.

pathologist
Pathologists perform autopsies to determine how and why a person died.

prosecution
Lawyers in a court of law who try to prove that the defendant carried out a crime.

serial killer
Someone who murders a number of people over a period of time, especially someone who uses the same method each time.

serologist
An expert in blood serum, the liquid part of blood.

sulfuric acid
A powerful, colorless, oily acid used in the manufacture of products such as fertilizers, explosives, detergents, and dyes.

superimpose
To place something on top of something else.

trace evidence
Small pieces of evidence found at a crime scene, such as hair, fiber, grass, glass, soil, blood spots, and skin.

ultraviolet
Radiation (energy waves) with wavelengths shorter than visible light but longer than x-rays.

x-ray
Radiation (energy waves) with wavelengths shorter than ultraviolet light. X-rays are mainly used in medicine to see inside the body.

FURTHER INFORMATION

BOOKS

CSI Expert!: Forensic Science for Kids by Karen K. Shulz (Prufrock Press, 2008)

Forensic Science by Chris Cooper (DK Publishing, 2008)

Gut-Eating Bugs: Maggots Reveal the Time of Death! by Danielle Denega (Franklin Watts, 2007)

Hair, Clothing, and Tire Track Evidence: Crime-Solving Science Experiments by Kenneth G. Rainis (Enslow Publishers, 2006)

WEB SITES

www.explainthatstuff.com/forensicscience.html
Explains forensic science and suggests activities to do at home.

www.fbi.gov/fbikids.htm
Web site set up by the FBI for children that shows what the agency does.

www.cyberbee.com/whodunnit/crime.html
Find out if you can follow the forensic clues and solve the crimes on this web site.

www.centredessciencesdemontreal.com/autopsy/index.htm
Play the award-winning forensics game, "Autopsy of a Murder," and use your forensic knowledge to solve the case.

INDEX

acid 12, 13, 14, 15
Allitt, Beverley 5
Amurao, Corazon 16–17, 19
Anderson, Gail 42
autopsies 9, 18, 32, 33

ballistics 31
Beattie, Bernard 8
bite mark 22, 23
blood 6, 7, 14, 18, 25, 32,
  33, 34, 35, 42
bone 13, 14, 26, 42
Brash, James Couper 10, 11
bullets 6, 14, 28, 30, 31
Bundy, Ted 20–23
Burke, William 4

Capone, Al 4
clothing 7, 37
comparison microscopes . . .21, 27
composite drawings 17, 20
computers 29, 31, 41
Crafts, Helle 24, 25
Crafts, Richard 24–27

DaRonch, Carol 21
dental records 6, 15, 20
dentures 13, 15
DNA 7, 33, 34, 35, 42, 43
DNA profiling 7
Durand-Deacon, Olive 13–15

Ellis, Ruth 5

fat 13, 14, 15
fibers 6, 25, 26, 27
fingerprints 6, 10, 18, 22, 28,
  29, 30, 33, 34

footprints 6, 29, 31, 32, 33
forensic anthropology 6, 42
forensic art 17, 20
forensic botanists 37
forensic dentistry 6, 23
forensic entomology 7, 11,
  38, 39, 42
forensic odontologists 6–7, 22,
  23

geographic profiling 40, 41
Glaister, John 10, 11

Haigh, John George 12–15
hair 6, 7, 21, 26, 32, 33, 42
Hare, William 4
Haskell, Neal 38
Henderson, Archibald 13
Henderson, Rose 13
human remains 6, 9, 10, 14,
  17, 20, 26, 41, 42

infrared spectrometry 27
insects 7, 11, 38, 39, 42

knife marks 6
Kray twins 5
Kuster, Roland 32, 33, 34, 35

Lee, Henry 25, 26
Levy, Lisa 22
luminal test 25

Mayo, Keith 24
McSwan, William 12
Minor, David 32, 34, 35

Neal, Kevin 36, 37, 38
Neary, Nita 22
Nilson, Dennis 5

paint .6
pathologists 7, 10, 32
photographs 10, 11, 17, 18,
  23, 32
Pickton, Robert 40–43

Ramirez, Richard 28–31
RFLP (restriction fragment length
  polymorphism) 34, 35
Richardson family 5
Rogerson, Mary 8, 9, 10, 11
Rossmo, Kim 40
Ruxton, Buck 8, 9, 11
Ruxton, Isabella 8, 9, 10

saliva .7
skeletons 6, 10
skin 7, 23
skulls 10, 11
soil 6
Souviron, Richard 22
Speck, Richard 16–19
striation marks 31
Sutcliffe, Peter 5

teeth 6, 22, 42, 43
teeth marks 7
time of death 7, 38, 39, 42
tire tracks 6
tissue 26
trace evidence 6

x-rays 10, 11